THIS BOOK BELONGS TO:

_____

_____

Shop our other books at
www.sillyslothpress.com

For questions and customer service, email us at
support@sillyslothpress.com

JOKE 1

Q: WHAT HAPPENED WHEN THE GRAPE GOT SQUISHED?

A: HE LET OUT A LITTLE WINE.

JOKE 2

I AM JUST SO GOOD AT SLEEPING.

I CAN DO IT WITH MY EYES CLOSED!

JOKE 3

Q: WHAT KIND OF CAR DOES A CHICKEN DRIVE?

A: A YOLKSWAGEN.

JOKE 4

NAME A KIND OF WATER THAT CAN'T FREEZE.

HOT WATER.

JOKE 5

Q: WHAT DO SANTA'S ELVES LISTEN TO AS THEY WORK?

A: WRAP MUSIC.

JOKE 6

Q: WHEN IS A DOOR NOT REALLY A DOOR?

A: WHEN IT'S AJAR.

JOKE 7

Q: WHAT GETS WETTER THE MORE IT DRIES?

A: A TOWEL.

JOKE 8

I DON'T PLAY SOCCER BECAUSE I'M GOOD AT IT.

I JUST DO IT FOR THE KICKS.

JOKE 9

"MY WIFE SUFFERS FROM A SERIOUS DRINKING PROBLEM."

"IS SHE AN ALCOHOLIC?"

"NO, BUT I AM! BUT SHE IS THE ONE WHO SUFFERS!"

JOKE 10

I AM ONLY FAMILIAR WITH 25/26 LETTERS OF THE ALPHABET.

I DO NOT KNOW WHY.

JOKE 11

Q: WHY DID THE WORKER GET FIRED FROM THE CRANBERRY JUICE FACTORY?

A: LACK OF CONCENTRATION.

JOKE 12

Q: WHY ARE ELEVATOR JOKES SO HILARIOUS?

A: THEY WORK ON SO MANY LEVELS.

JOKE 13

WOW SO MUCH HAS CHANGED SINCE MY GIRLFRIEND GOT PREGNANT.

FOR EXAMPLE- MY NAME, ADDRESS, AND PHONE NUMBER!

JOKE 14

Q: WHAT IS A LAZY PERSON'S FAVORITE EXERCISE?

A: DIDDLY SQUATS!

JOKE 15

Q: WHY WAS IT RUDE FOR A SNOWMAN TO PICK A CARROT?

A: BECAUSE HE WAS PICKING HIS NOSE!

JOKE 16

Q: WHAT DID THE PAPA CHIMNEY SAY TO THE BABY CHIMNEY?

A: YOU ARE TOO YOUNG TO BE SMOKING!

JOKE 17

Q: WHY WERE THE KITCHEN UTENSILS STUCK TOGETHER?

A: BECAUSE THEY WERE SPOONING.

JOKE 18

Q: WHAT IS THE BEST THING TO DO WHEN YOU SEE A SPACEMAN?

A: PARK IN IT!

JOKE 19

Q: WHY DO GHOSTS RIDE IN ELEVATORS?

A: BECAUSE IT LIFTS THEIR SPIRITS.

JOKE 20

Q: WHAT DOES IT SOUND LIKE WHEN A COW BREAKS THE SOUND BARRIER?

A: COW-BOOM!

JOKE 21

Q: WHERE DID THE COMPUTER GO DANCING?

A: THE DISC-O!

JOKE 22

Q: WHY WAS 6 AFRAID OF 7?

A: BECAUSE 7-8-9.

JOKE 23

DON'T WORRY, YOU AREN'T COMPLETELY USELESS.

YOU CAN ALWAYS SERVE AS A BAD EXAMPLE.

JOKE 24

Q: WHAT IS THE BEST WAY TO WATCH A FLY-FISHING TOURNAMENT?

A: LIVE STREAM.

JOKE 25

DAUGHTER: DAD, I'M HUNGRY!

DAD: HI HUNGRY, I'M DAD.

JOKE 26

Q: WHY DID THE JELLYBEAN WANT TO GO TO SCHOOL?

A: TO BECOME A SMARTIE.

JOKE 27

Q: WHAT DID THE BASEBALL CAP SAY TO THE SOMBRERO?

A: YOU STAY HERE, I'LL GO ON AHEAD

JOKE 28

Q: WHAT KINDS OF PICTURES DO OYSTERS TAKE?

A: SHELLFIES.

JOKE 29

Q: HOW DO YOU KEEP A BAGEL FROM RUNNING AWAY?

A: LOX IT UP.

JOKE 30

Q: WHERE DO COWS GO ON A DATE?

A: THE MOO-VIES.

JOKE 31

Q: WHAT HAPPENS WHEN A FROG'S TRUCK DIES?

A: HE GETS A JUMP. AND IF THAT DOESN'T WORK, HE HAS TO GET TOAD.

JOKE 32

Q: DO YOU KNOW THE BEST WAY TO MAKE SOMEONE CURIOUS?

A: I'LL TELL YOU TOMORROW!

JOKE 33

Q: WHY ARE DOGS SUCH BAD STORYTELLERS?

A: BECAUSE THEY ONLY HAVE ONE TALE.

JOKE 34

Q: WHY WAS THE NOSE MAD AT THE FINGER?

A: BECAUSE HE WAS ALWAYS PICKING ON HIM!

JOKE 35

Q: HOW CAN YOU STOP AN ASTRONAUT'S BABY FROM CRYING?

A: YOU JUST ROCKET!

JOKE 36

Q: WHAT DO YOU CALL A MOUNTAIN WHO WANTS TO BE A COMEDIAN?

A: HILL-ARIOUS.

JOKE 37

Q: WHAT IS A TORNADO'S FAVORITE GAME?

A: TWISTER!

JOKE 38

Q: I HAVE EIGHTEEN EYES, TWENTY TEETH, AND A VERY LONG NOSE. WHAT AM I?

A: UGLY.

JOKE 39

Q: HOW DO YOU MAKE A TISSUE DANCE?

A: PUT A LITTLE BOOGIE IN IT!

JOKE 40

Q: WHAT DO YOU CALL A FLOWER THAN RUNS ON ELECTRICITY?

A: A POWER PLANT.

JOKE 41

Q: WHY IS IT DIFFICULT TO EXPLAIN JOKES TO KLEPTOMANIACS?

A: BECAUSE THEY ARE ALWAYS TAKING THINGS, LITERALLY.

JOKE 42

Q: WHY CAN'T YOU HEAR A PTERODACTYL USING THE BATHROOM?

A: BECAUSE THE 'P' IS SILENT.

JOKE 43

I WAS TOLD I SHOULD WRITE A BOOK.

WHAT A NOVEL CONCEPT.

JOKE 44

Q: WHAT TIME DID THE DAD GO TO THE DENTIST?

A: TOOTH HURT-y.

JOKE 45

Q: DO YOU KNOW HOW POPULAR THAT CEMETERY IS?

A: PEOPLE ARE JUST DYING TO GET IN THERE!

JOKE 46

Q: WHAT KIND OF TREE FITS IN YOUR HAND?

A: A PALM TREE!

JOKE 47

Q: WHAT DID THE TONSIL SAY TO THE ADENOID?

A: GET DRESSED, THE DOCTOR IS TAKING US OUT!

JOKE 48

Q: WHERE DO BABY CATS LEARN HOW TO SWIM?

A: THE KITTY POOL.

JOKE 49

Q: WHAT IS THE BEST PRESENT EVER?

A: A BUSTED DRUM. YOU CAN'T BEAT IT!

JOKE 50

Q: HOW DO ATTORNEYS SAY GOODBYE?

A: "WE'LL BE SUING YOU!"

JOKE 51

Q: WHEN DOES A JOKE BECOME A DAD JOKE?

A: WHEN IT BECOMES APPARENT.

JOKE 52

Q: WHY DID THE PAPER TOWEL ROLL DOWNHILL?

A: TO GET TO THE BOTTOM.

JOKE 53

Q: WHAT DID ONE DORITO FARMER SAY TO THE OTHER?

A: COOL RANCH!

JOKE 54

Q: WHY DON'T GHOSTS GO TRICK OR TREATING?

A: BECAUSE THEY HAVE NO BODY TO GO WITH.

JOKE 55

Q: WHICH DAY DO CHICKENS DREAD?

A: FRI-DAY.

JOKE 56

Q: WHY DID THE WOMAN GET FIRED FROM THE CALENDAR FACTORY?

A: BECAUSE SHE TOOK A FEW DAYS OFF.

JOKE 57

Q: CAN A GRASSHOPPER JUMP HIGHER THAN A HOUSE?

A: OF COURSE! HOUSES CAN'T JUMP.

JOKE 58

ONE COMPANY OWNER IS TALKING WITH ANOTHER.

"HOW DO YOU GET ALL OF YOUR EMPLOYEES TO WORK ON TIME?"

"IT'S EASY! 40 EMPLOYEES, 30 PARKING SPACES!"

JOKE 59

GYM TEACHER'S FAMOUS LAST WORD:

"ALL SPEARS TO ME!"

JOKE 60

Q: HOW MANY APPLES GROW ON A TREE?

A: ALL OF THEM.

JOKE 61

CUSTOMER: I AM OUTRAGED!
THERE IS A HAIR IN MY SOUP!

WAITER: AT THIS PRICE,
WHAT DID YOU EXPECT?
A WHOLE WIG?

JOKE 62

Q: WHERE DID THE NEWLYWED
BUNNIES GO AFTER THEIR
WEDDING?

A: ON A BUNNY-MOON!

JOKE 63

Q: WHY DID THE BANK GET
BORED?

A: BECAUSE IT LOST INTEREST.

JOKE 64

SON: DAD, WHAT IS AN ALCOHOLIC?

DAD: DO YOU SEE THOSE 4 TREES? AN ALCOHOLIC WOULD SEE 8.

SON: BUT THERE ARE ONLY 2 TREES.

JOKE 65

I HAVE A SERIOUS ELEVATOR PHOBIA.

SO, I TAKE STEPS TO AVOID THEM.

JOKE 66

Q: WHAT DO YOU CALL A FIBBING KITTY?

A: FELINE.

JOKE 67

Q: WHAT IS INVISIBLE AND SMELLS LIKE WORMS?

A: A BIRD'S FART.

JOKE 68

DOCTOR: YOUR TEST RESULTS SHOW THAT YOU WILL LIVE TO BE 70.

PATIENT: BUT I JUST TURNED 70.

DOCTOR: I KNOW, I TOLD YOU TO TAKE BETTER CARE OF YOURSELF!

JOKE 69

Q: WHY SHOULD YOU AVOID EATING A WATCH?

A: BECAUSE IT'S TOO TIME CONSUMING.

JOKE 70

Q: WHAT IS THE MOST PATRIOTIC SPORT?

A: FLAG FOOTBALL.

JOKE 71

Q: WHY DID THE BICYCLE FALL ASLEEP?

A: IT WAS TWO-TIRED.

JOKE 72

Q: HAVE YOU HEARD ABOUT CORDUROY PILLOWS?

A: THEY ARE MAKING HEADLINES.

JOKE 73

Q: HAVE YOU HEARD ABOUT THE NAKED WOMAN WHO ROBS BANKS?

A: NOBODY CAN REMEMBER HER FACE!

JOKE 74

Q: HOW DO YOU KNOW IF THERE IS AN ELEPHANT UNDER YOUR BED?

A: YOUR HEAD HITS THE CEILING!

JOKE 75

Q: WHAT TIME IS IT WHEN A CLOCK STRIKES 13?

A: TIME TO GET A NEW CLOCK!

JOKE 76

Q: WHAT DOES A BABY COMPUTER CALL ITS FATHER?

A: DATA.

JOKE 77

Q: WHY WAS THE ALGEBRA BOOK DEPRESSED?

A: IT WAS FULL OF PROBLEMS.

JOKE 78

Q: WHAT DID THE PILLOW SAY WHEN IT FELL OFF THE BED?

A: OH SHEET!

JOKE 79

Q: WHAT DO YOU CALL A DROID THAT TAKES THE SCENIC ROUTE?

A: R2 DETOUR.

JOKE 80

Q: WHAT DO YOU CALL A MINIATURE PONY WITH A SORE THROAT?

A: A LITTLE HOARSE.

JOKE 81

Q: WHAT DO YOU CALL A BLIND DINOSAUR?

A: A DO-YOU-THINK-HE-SAW-US.

JOKE 82

Q: HOW DOES AN ESKIMO BUILD A HOUSE?

A: IGLOOS IT TOGETHER.

JOKE 83

Q: WHY DID THE POLICEMAN SMEAR PEANUT BUTTER ON THE ROAD?

A: TO GO WITH THE TRAFFIC JAM!

JOKE 84

Q: WHY ARE DOCTORS SO CALM?

A: BECAUSE THEY HAVE A LOT OF PATIENTS.

JOKE 85

Q: WHAT KIND OF MUSIC DO ALIENS LISTEN TO?

A: NEP-TUNES.

JOKE 86

ONCE I MET A GIRL WHO HAD 12 NIPPLES.

SOUNDS FREAKY, DOZEN TIT.

JOKE 87

IF A TODDLER REFUSES TO GO TO SLEEP, ARE THEY GUILTY OF RESISTING A REST?

JOKE 88

Q: WHAT DID THE BABY CORN SAY WHEN HIS DAD WENT TO WORK?

A: WHERE IS POPCORN?

JOKE 89

Q: WHY ARE BASKETBALL PLAYERS DIFFICULT TO DINE WITH?

A: BECAUSE THEY ARE CONSTANTLY DRIBBLING.

JOKE 90

YESTERDAY MY WIFE ASKED ME FOR SOME LIPSTICK.

I ACCIDENTLY GAVE HER A GLUE STICK AND SHE STILL ISN'T TALKING TO ME.

JOKE 91

Q: WHAT DO YOU CALL AN INCREDIBLY OLD SNOWMAN?

A: WATER.

JOKE 92

DOCTOR: HELLO. DO YOU HAVE AN EYE PROBLEM?

PATIENT: WOW! YES, HOW DID YOU KNOW?

DOCTOR: WELL YOU CAME IN THROUGH THE WINDOW INSTEAD OF THE DOOR.

JOKE 93

Q: WHY DO FISH LIVE IN SALT WATER?

A: BECAUSE PEPPER MAKES THEM SNEEZE!

JOKE 94

I USED TO HATE FACIAL HAIR.

BUT THEN IT GREW ON ME.

JOKE 95

Q: WHAT DID THE FISHERMAN SAY WHEN HE ATE THE CLOWNFISH?

A: THAT TASTED A LITTLE FUNNY.

JOKE 96

Q: WHY DID THE CHIMPANZEE FALL OUT OF THE TREE?

A: IT WAS DEAD.

JOKE 97

A FAMISHED TERMITE WALKS INTO A BAR.

HE SAYS, "WHERE IS THE BAR TENDER?"

JOKE 98

Q: WHY ARE GHOSTS THE WORST LIARS?

A: BECAUSE YOU CAN SEE RIGHT THROUGH THEM.

JOKE 99

Q: WHAT DID THE MOUNTAIN SAY TO THE BLUFF?

A: HEY CLIFF!

JOKE 100

Q: WHAT DO YOU CALL AN AMERICAN BEE?

A: A USB.

JOKE 101

Q: WHY CAN'T A HAND BE 12 INCHES LONG?

A: BECAUSE THEN IT WOULD BE A FOOT.

JOKE 102

Q: WHAT DID THE PLATE SAY TO THE CUP?

A: DINNER IS ON ME!

JOKE 103

WHOEVER INVENTED AUTOCORRECT IS A MASSHOLE.

HE CAN DUCK RIGHT OFF.

JOKE 104

Q: HAVE YOU HEARD ABOUT THE MAN WHO INVENTED THE KNOCK KNOCK JOKE?

A: HE WAS GIVEN THE NO-BELL PRIZE.

JOKE 105

Q: WHAT IS GREEN, POPULAR, AND SINGS?

A: ELVIS PARSLEY.

JOKE 106

Q: WHY IS 288 NEVER MENTIONED?

A: IT'S TWO GROSS.

JOKE 107

Q: WHAT KIND OF SHOES DO NINJAS WEAR?

A: SNEAKERS.

JOKE 108

Q: WHAT DO YOU CALL QUESO THAT DOESN'T BELONG TO YOU?

A: NACHO CHEESE.

JOKE 109

Q: WHAT IS THE BEST WAY TO IMPRESS A SQUIRREL?

A: ACT LIKE A NUT.

JOKE 110

I WAS FIRED FROM THE BANK TODAY.

A WOMAN ASKED ME TO CHECK HER BALANCE, SO I PUSHED HER OVER.

JOKE 111

Q: WHAT TYPE OF TEA IS THE HARDEST TO SWALLOW?

A: REALITY.

JOKE 112

Q: WHAT DID THE FLOOR SAY TO THE WALL?

A: MEET ME AT THE CORNER.

JOKE 113

Q: WHAT DO YOU GET A MAN WITH THE HEART OF A LION?

A: BANNED FROM THE ZOO.

JOKE 114

Q: WHAT DOES A HOUSE WEAR ON A DATE?

A: ADDRESS.

JOKE 115

Q: WHAT DO YOU CALL A MAN WHOSE BRIEFCASE IS IN A TREE?

A: A BRANCH MANAGER.

JOKE 116

Q: WHAT DO YOU CALL A DOG THAT DOESN'T HAVE LEGS?

A: WHATEVER YOU WANT, HE'S STILL NOT COMING.

JOKE 117

Q: WHY DON'T YOU EVER SEE HIPPOS HIDING IN TREES?

A: BECAUSE THEY ARE EXCEPTIONALLY GOOD AT IT!

JOKE 118

Q: WHAT HAPPENS WHEN YOU CROSS A GREAT WHITE AND A DOG?

A: A TERRIFIED MAILMAN.

JOKE 119

Q: HAVE YOU HEARD THE RUMOR ABOUT JELLY?

A: WELL, I'M NOT GOING TO SPREAD IT!

JOKE 120

Q: WHY ARE DINOSAURS SO QUIET?

A: BECAUSE THEY ARE DEAD.

JOKE 121

Q: WHY DID THE BANK ROBBER HIDE HIS MONEY IN THE FREEZER?

A: HE WANTED COLD HARD CASH.

JOKE 122

STOP LOOKING FOR THE PERFECT MATCH.

JUST USE A LIGHTER.

JOKE 123

Q: WHAT DO YOU CALL A DANGEROUS SUN SHOWER?

A: A RAIN OF TERROR!

JOKE 124

Q: WHAT DID THE TEA REPORT TO THE POLICE?

A: A MUGGING.

JOKE 125

Q: WHAT DO YOU CALL A DEAD ALMOND?

A: DIAMOND.

JOKE 126

A LABORING WOMAN STARTED SHOUTING, "SHOULDN'T! WOULDN'T! CAN'T! DON'T!"

BUT THE MIDWIFE WASN'T WORRIED. IT WAS JUST CONTRACTIONS.

JOKE 127

Q: HOW DO ASTRONAUTS ORGANIZE A SURPRISE PARTY?

A: **THEY PLANET.**

JOKE 128

MEN 1820: I KILLED A BUFFALO.

MEN 1920: I FIXED THE ROOF.

MEN 2020: I SHAVED MY LEGS.

JOKE 129

Q: WHAT DO SEA MONSTERS EAT FOR A SNACK?

A: **FISH AND SHIPS.**

JOKE 130

Q: WHY IS THE BANK SO BAD AT KEEPING SECRETS?

A: BECAUSE IT HAS SO MANY TELLERS.

JOKE 131

Q: WHAT DID THE JANITOR SAY WHEN HE JUMPED OUT OF THE CLOSET?

A: SUPPLIES!

JOKE 132

NAME AN ANIMAL THAT IS ALWAYS AT A BASEBALL GAME.

A BAT.

JOKE 133

PERSONALLY, I DON'T TRUST STAIRS.

THEY ARE ALWAYS UP TO SOMETHING.

JOKE 134

Q: WHAT HAPPENS WHEN YOU PAMPER A DAIRY COW?

A: SPOILED MILK.

JOKE 135

Q: WHAT DID ONE MARIJUANA PLANT SAY TO THE OTHER?

A: HEY BUD.

JOKE 136

Q: WHAT DO YOU CALL A FACTORY THAT SELLS PASSABLE PRODUCTS?

A: SATISFACTORY!

JOKE 137

Q: WHAT DO YOU CALL A BABY MONKEY?

A: A CHIMP OFF THE OLD BLOCK.

JOKE 138

HEY DAD, DID YOU GET A HAIRCUT?

NOPE! I GOT THEM ALL CUT!

JOKE 139

Q: WHAT DO YOU CALL AN ELEPHANT THAT DOESN'T MATTER?

A: AN IRRELEPHANT.

JOKE 140

Q: WHICH PIECE OF SCHOOL SUPPLIES IS IN CHARGE?

A: THE RULER.

JOKE 141

Q: WHAT IS THE BEST WAY TO CARVE WOOD?

A: WHITTLE BY WHITTLE.

JOKE 142

Q: WHY COULDN'T THE DELIVERY MAN MAIL ANY ENVELOPES?

A: THEY WERE ALL STATIONARY.

JOKE 143

Q: WHAT IS THE BEST THING ABOUT LIVING IN SWITZERLAND?

A: I HAVE NO IDEA! BUT THE FLAG IS A BIG PLUS!

JOKE 144

Q: WHAT DID THE NOTEPAD SAY TO THE PENCIL?

A: YOU HAVE A GOOD POINT!

JOKE 145

Q: WHY DO GEOLOGISTS LOVE THEIR JOBS?

A: THEY'RE NEVER TAKEN FOR GRANITE.

JOKE 146

Q: WHY DID THE ORANGE LOSE THE RACE?

A: IT RAN OUT OF JUICE.

JOKE 147

Q: WHY WAS THE SUBSTITUTE TEACHER WEARING SUNGLASSES?

A: BECAUSE THE STUDENTS WERE SO BRIGHT!

JOKE 148

I THOUGHT ABOUT GOING ON AN ALL-CASHEW BASED DIET.

BUT THAT IS JUST NUTS!

JOKE 149

Q: WHY DID THE PRO GOLFER NEED NEW SOCKS?

A: BECAUSE HE GOT A HOLE IN ONE.

JOKE 150

Q: HOW DO BEES STYLE THEIR HAIR?

A: WITH A HONEYCOMB.

JOKE 151

WIFE: HONEY, CAN YOU PLEASE PUT THE CAT OUT?

HUSBAND: I DIDN'T KNOW IT WAS ON FIRE!

JOKE 152

Q: WHAT DO YOU CALL A TOOTHLESS PANDA?

A: A GUMMY BEAR.

JOKE 153

PATIENT: HEY DOC, I AM SO NERVOUS! THIS IS MY FIRST SURGERY.

DOCTOR: DON'T WORRY. MINE TOO!

JOKE 154

PRO TIP: DON'T BUY ANYTHING WITH VELCRO.

IT'S A TOTAL RIP-OFF!

JOKE 155

MY BOSS TOLD ME TO HAVE A NICE DAY.

SO, I WENT HOME.

JOKE 156

I JUST SAW THE MOST EMOTIONAL WEDDING.

EVEN THE CAKES WERE IN TIERS!

JOKE 157

Q: WHAT HAS TWO BUTTS AND KILLS PEOPLE?

A: AN ASSASSIN.

JOKE 158

Q: WHY DID THE SINGER TAKE A WHEELBARROW TO CHOIR PRACTICE?

A: SHE NEEDED SOMETHING TO CARRY A TUNE.

JOKE 159

Q: WHAT IS THE DIFFERENCE BETWEEN A NUMERATOR AND A DENOMINATOR?

A: A SHORT LINE. (ONLY A FRACTION OF PEOPLE WILL UNDERSTAND THIS).

JOKE 160

THE DIRECTIONS SAID, "SET THE OVEN TO 180 DEGREES."

OK. BUT NOW I CAN'T EVEN OPEN THE DOOR BECAUSE IT IS FACING THE WALL.

JOKE 161

Q: HOW DO YOU ROB A SNOWMAN?

A: WITH A HAIRDRYER.

JOKE 162

Q: WHAT SHOULD AN ALCOHOLIC BIRD DO?

A: GO TO TWEETMENT.

JOKE 163

NOT TO BRAG, BUT I FINISHED THE PUZZLE IN A WEEK.

IT SAYS 2-4 YEARS ON THE BOX.

JOKE 164

I GOT SOME SHOES FROM A DRUG DEALER.

I HAVE NO IDEA WHAT HE LACED THEM WITH, BUT I HAVE BEEN TRIPPING ALL DAY!

JOKE 165

Q: WHAT IS FORREST GUMP'S E-MAIL PASSWORD?

A: 1-FORREST-1.

JOKE 166

ISN'T IT WEIRD HOW PLASTIC SURGERY USED TO BE SO TABOO?

BUT NOW WITH BOTOX, NO ONE RAISES AN EYEBROW!

JOKE 167

Q: WHY ARE SPIDERS SO SMART?

A: THEY HAVE FULL ACCESS TO THE WEB.

JOKE 168

Q: WHAT IS THE MOST DETAIL-ORIENTED BODY OF WATER?

A: THE PACIFIC OCEAN.

JOKE 169

HAVE YOU HEARD ABOUT THE SEAMSTRESS WHO FELL INTO THE UPHOLSTERY MACHINE?

SHE IS FULLY RECOVERED.

JOKE 170

TO THE PERSON WHO BROKE MY GLASSES:

I WILL FIND YOU. I HAVE CONTACTS.

JOKE 171

Q: WHY DID THE COMPUTER GO TO THE HOSPITAL?

A: IT CAME DOWN WITH A VIRUS.

JOKE 172

Q: WHAT IS A TAPESTRY MAKER'S FAVORITE DANCE MOVE?

A: CUTTING A RUG.

JOKE 173

A WIFE CAUGHT HER HUSBAND STANDING ON A SCALE AND SUCKING IN HIS STOMACH. "THAT DOESN'T HELP," SHE SAID.

HE REPLIED, "OF COURSE, IT DOES! HOW ELSE WILL I SEE THE NUMBERS?"

JOKE 174

Q: WHAT DO YOU CALL SOMEONE WITH NO BODY AND NO NOSE?

A: NOBODY KNOWS.

JOKE 175

Q: WHAT DID THE SODA CAN CALL HIS FATHER?

A: POP

JOKE 176

Q: WHY WAS CINDERELLA CUT FROM THE BASEBALL TEAM?

A: BECAUSE SHE RAN AWAY FROM THE BALL.

JOKE 177

Q: WHAT IS FASTER- HOT OR COLD?

A: HOT! WHY? BECAUSE YOU CAN CATCH A COLD!

JOKE 178

Q: WHAT DID THE POLICEMAN SAY TO HIS BELLY?

A: YOU'RE UNDER A VEST!

JOKE 179

SUNDAYS ARE ALWAYS A LITTLE DEPRESSING, BUT THE DAY BEFORE IS A SADDER DAY.

JOKE 180

Q: WHY SHOULDN'T EGGS TELL JOKES?

A: THEY WOULD CRACK THEMSELVES UP!

JOKE 181

Q: WHAT DO GHOULS EAT FOR DESSERT?

A: I-SCREAM.

JOKE 182

I WOULD AVOID THE SUSHI IF I WERE YOU.

IT'S A LITTLE FISHY.

JOKE 183

Q: WHERE DO FISH DEPOSIT THEIR MONEY?

A: IN A RIVERBANK.

JOKE 184

I COULD TELL A JOKE ABOUT MACARONI.

BUT IT'S A LITTLE CHEESY.

JOKE 185

Q: WANT TO HEAR A JOKE ABOUT CRYING?

A: NEVER MIND. IT'S TEARABLE.

JOKE 186

Q: WHAT DO YOU CALL A GUY WHO IS FOUND LYING ON YOUR DOORSTEP?

A: MATT.

JOKE 187

IF TWO VEGETARIANS GET INTO A BRAWL, IS IT STILL CONSIDERED A BEEF?

JOKE 188

IF THE EARLY BIRD GETS THE WORM, THEN I WILL SLEEP UNTIL THERE ARE WAFFLES.

JOKE 189

Q: WHAT DOES A SPIDER BRIDE WEAR ON HER BIG DAY?

A: A WEBBING DRESS.

JOKE 190

I DID MY BEST TO CATCH THE FOG.

BUT I MIST IT.

JOKE 191

Q: WHY DID THE JELLY DONUT GO TO THE DENTIST?

A: BECAUSE HE LOST HIS FILLING.

JOKE 192

Q: WHAT DID ONE LEGUME SAY TO THE OTHER?

A: HOW YOU BEAN?

JOKE 193

Q: WHAT TYPE OF BUILDING HAS THE MOST STORIES?

A: THE LIBRARY!

JOKE 194

Q: WHAT IS IT CALLED WHEN YOU CROSS A SNOWMAN WITH A VAMPIRE?

A: FROSTBITE.

JOKE 195

Q: HOW DO SNAILS FIGHT?

A: THEY SLUG IT OUT.

JOKE 196

I ENTERED A PUN CONTEST.

I SUBMITTED TEN, FIGURING AT LEAST ONE WOULD WIN.

BUT NO PUN IN TEN DID.

JOKE 197

Q: HOW CAN A CHEETAH CHANGE HIS SPOTS?

A: BY MOVING.

JOKE 198

Q: WHAT IS AN ASTRONAUT'S FAVORITE PART OF A COMPUTER KEYBOARD?

A: THE SPACE BAR.

JOKE 199

Q: WHAT DID THE RING FINGER SAY TO THE PINKY?

A: I'M IN GLOVE WITH YOU.

JOKE 200

Q: WHERE DOES A STEAK GO TO DANCE?

A: THE MEAT-BALL.

JOKE 201

Q: WHO IS A GHOST'S TRUE LOVE?

A: HIS GHOUL-FRIEND.

JOKE 202

Q: WHAT HAPPENS WHEN YOU HAVE A BLADDER INFECTION?

A: URINE TROUBLE.

JOKE 203

Q: WHY CAN'T YOU TRUST BALLOONS?

A: BECAUSE THEY ARE FULL OF HOT AIR.

JOKE 204

Q: HOW CAN YOU IDENTIFY A DOGWOOD TREE?

A: FROM THE BARK.

JOKE 205

Q: WHAT DID THE DIGITAL CLOCK SAY TO THE GRANDFATHER CLOCK?

A: LOOK! NO HANDS!

JOKE 206

Q: WHAT KIND OF MUSIC DO WINDMILLS LIKE?

A: THEY ARE METAL FANS.

JOKE 207

Q: WHY DON'T CLAMS DONATE TO CHARITY?

A: BECAUSE THEY ARE SHELLFISH.

JOKE 208

Q: WHAT IS THE DIFFERENCE BETWEEN A CAT AND A COMMA?

A: A CAT HAS CLAWS AT THE END OF ITS PAWS. A COMMA HAS A PAUSE AT THE END OF ITS CLAUSE.

JOKE 209

Q: WHAT DID THE VOLCANO SAY TO HIS GIRLFRIEND?

A: I LAVA YOU!

JOKE 210

Q: WHY DO SEAGULLS FLY OVER THE SEA?

A: BECAUSE IF THEY FLEW OVER THE BAY THEN THEY WOULD BE BAGELS!

JOKE 211

I STARTED READING THIS HORROR STORY IN BRAILLE.

SOMETHING BAD IS GOING TO HAPPEN. I CAN FEEL IT.

JOKE 212

Q: WHAT IS THE BEST WAY TO COMMUNICATE WITH A TROUT?

A: DROP IT A LINE.

JOKE 213

Q: WHY DID THE CAN CRUSHER QUIT HIS JOB?

A: BECAUSE IT WAS SODA PRESSING!

JOKE 214

Q: HOW DO WRITERS SAY HELLO?

A: HEY, HAVEN'T WE METAPHOR?

JOKE 215

Q: WHY DO YOU CARRY SO MUCH LOOSE CHANGE?

A: NO ONE CAN SAY I LACK COMMON SENSE.

JOKE 216

SON TO MOM: THE KIDS ARE LAUGHING AT ME AND SAYING MY TEETH ARE TOO LONG!

MOM TO SON: OH HUSH! LOOK NOW YOU HAVE SCRATCHED THE FLOOR AGAIN!

JOKE 217

Q: WHY IS A CALCULATOR SO RELIABLE?

A: YOU CAN COUNT ON IT!

JOKE 218

Q: WHY DID THE POTATO GO TO THE DENTIST?

A: IT NEEDED A ROOT CANAL.

JOKE 219

I BROKE MY ARM IN TWO PLACES.

MY DOCTOR TOLD ME TO STOP GOING TO THOSE PLACES!

JOKE 220

Q: NAME A ROOM WITH NO DOORS THAT NOBODY CAN ENTER.

A: A MUSHROOM!

JOKE 221

Q: WHAT DO ELVES LEARN IN KINDERGARTEN?

A: THE ELF-ABET.

JOKE 222

Q: DO YOU KNOW THE LEAST SPOKEN LANGUAGE IN THE ENTIRE WORLD?

A: SIGN LANGUAGE.

JOKE 223

WIFE: I'M ADDICTED TO TWITTER!

HUSBAND: SORRY, I DON'T FOLLOW.

JOKE 224

Q: WHY DO MALE ANTS FLOAT?

A: BECAUSE THEY ARE BUOY-ANT.

JOKE 225

I JUST HATE IT WHEN PEOPLE SAY AGE IS JUST A NUMBER.

AGE IS CLEARLY A WORD!

JOKE 226

TWO FISH ARE IN A TANK.

ONE ASKS THE OTHER, "HOW THE HECK DO YOU DRIVE THIS THING?"

JOKE 227

Q: WHY DID THE BELT GET ARRESTED?

A: BECAUSE HE HELD UP A PAIR OF PANTS.

JOKE 228

Q: WHAT DO YOU CALL A BULL WITH NO LEGS?

A: GROUND BEEF.

JOKE 229

Q: WHERE DO CRAYONS GO TO ON VACATION?

A: COLOR-ADO.

JOKE 230

Q: WHAT DID THE UNDERWEAR SAY TO THE TROUSERS?

A: WHAT'S UP BRITCHES?!

JOKE 231

I USED TO WORK IN THE SHOE-REPAIR BUSINESS.

I HAD TO QUIT BECAUSE IT WAS SOLE DESTROYING!

JOKE 232

Q: WHAT DO YOU CALL A DOG MAGICIAN?

A: A LABRACADABRADOR.

JOKE 233

Q: WHY DO DIVERS FALL BACKWARDS OFF THE BOAT?

A: BECAUSE IF THEY FELL FORWARDS, THEY WOULD STILL BE ON THE BOAT!

JOKE 234

I SPLURGED ON AN EXPENSIVE NEW BELT, BUT IT DOESN'T FIT.

WHAT A WAIST.

JOKE 235

Q: WHAT IS ONE OF THE WORST THINGS ABOUT BEING LONELY?

A: PLAYING FRISBEE.

JOKE 236

Q: WHY DO ACTORS SAY, "BREAK A LEG?"

A: BECAUSE THEY ARE PART OF A CAST.

JOKE 237

Q: WHAT DOES THE PAINTER DO WHEN THE TEMPERATURE DROPS?

A: HE PUTS ON ANOTHER COAT.

JOKE 238

Q: WHY DID THE PHOTOGRAPH GO TO JAIL?

A: BECAUSE IT WAS FRAMED.

JOKE 239

Q: WHAT DID THE BUDDHIST MONK SAY AT THE HOT DOG STAND?

A: MAKE ME ONE WITH EVERYTHING.

JOKE 240

Q: WHAT DO YOU CALL A GROUP OF DISORGANIZED FELINES?

A: CAT-TASTROPHE.

JOKE 241

Q: WHAT DID THE PIRATE CAPTAIN SAY ON HIS 80TH BIRTHDAY?

A: AYE MATEY!

JOKE 242

Q: HOW DID THE HIPSTER DROWN?

A: MAINSTREAM.

JOKE 243

Q: HOW DO YOU GET A COUNTRY GIRL'S ATTENTION?

A: A TRACTOR.

JOKE 244

MY DOG USED TO CHASE PEOPLE ON A BIKE ALL DAY.

IT GOT SO BAD THAT I FINALLY HAD TO TAKE HIS BIKE AWAY!

JOKE 245

JUSTICE IS A DISH THAT IS BEST SERVED COLD.

IF IT WERE SERVED WARM, THEN IT WOULD BE JUSTWATER.

JOKE 246

Q: WHY DID THE SCARECROW GET AN AWARD?

A: HE WAS OUTSTANDING IN HIS FIELD.

JOKE 247

Q: WHAT KIND OF DINOSAUR LOVES NAPS?

A: STEGA-SNORE-US.

JOKE 248

Q: WHAT DID THE BUFFALO SAY WHEN HIS SON LEFT?

A: BISON!

JOKE 249

Q: WHAT IS BROWN AND STICKY?

A: A STICK.

JOKE 250

WIFE: I AM WORRIED ABOUT MY HUSBAND. AFTER HE FINISHES HIS COFFEE, HE EATS THE MUG. ALL THAT IS LEFT IS THE HANDLE!

DOCTOR: HOW WEIRD. THE HANDLE IS THE BEST PART!

JOKE 251

Q: HAVE YOU HEARD ABOUT THE PENCIL WITH TWO ERASERS?

A: IT WAS POINTLESS.

JOKE 252

Q: WHAT IS THE LOUDEST PET YOU CAN HAVE?

A: A TRUM-PET.

JOKE 253

I FINALLY DECIDED TO SELL MY VACUUM CLEANER.

IT WAS JUST GATHERING DUST!

JOKE 254

Q: WHY DID THE MELONS GET MARRIED?

A: BECAUSE THEY CANTALOUPE.

JOKE 255

Q: HAVE YOU HEARD ABOUT THE MATH TEACHER WHO WAS AFRAID OF NEGATIVE NUMBERS?

A: HE WOULD STOP AT NOTHING TO AVOID THEM!

JOKE 256

Q: WHAT DO YOU CALL AN ALLIGATOR WHO WEARS A VEST AND FIGHTS CRIME?

A: AN INVESTIGATOR.

JOKE 257

Q: WHAT IS THE ALL-TIME NUMBER ONE CAUSE OF DIVORCE?

A: MARRIAGE.

JOKE 258

DON'T WORRY IF A BIRD POOPS ON YOUR HEAD.

BE HAPPY THAT DOGS CAN'T FLY!

JOKE 259

Q: HOW WAS THE PAINT THIEF APPREHENDED?

A: HE WAS CAUGHT RED HANDED.

JOKE 260

Q: HOW CAN A SCIENTIST MAKE SURE HER BREATH IS FRESH?

A: WITH EXPERI-MINTS!

JOKE 261

Q: WHY DID THE BABY COOKIE START CRYING?

A: BECAUSE ITS PARENTS WERE A WAFER SO LONG.

JOKE 262

Q: HOW DO METEOROLOGISTS REACH THE TOP OF A MOUNTAIN?

A: THEY CLIMATE.

JOKE 263

Q: DO YOU KNOW WHAT'S UP?

A: THE SKY.

JOKE 264

Q: WHAT HAPPENS WHEN YOU WITNESS A SHIPWRECK?

A: YOU LET IT SINK IN.

JOKE 265

HAVING TROUBLE SLEEPING? I RECOMMEND CUTTING THE LEGS OF YOUR BED.

YOU WILL SLEEP DEEPER.

JOKE 266

I TOLD MY PCP I HEARD BUZZING.

HE SAID, "IT'S JUST A BUG GOING AROUND."

JOKE 267

Q: WHY DID THE INVISIBLE WOMAN TURN DOWN THE JOB?

A: SHE JUST COULDN'T SEE HERSELF DOING IT.

JOKE 268

I JUST WROTE A BOOK ON REVERSE PSYCHOLOGY.

WHATEVER YOU DO, DO *NOT* READ IT!

JOKE 269

MY DAUGHTER ASKED, "CAN I HAVE A BOOKMARK?"

I BURST INTO TEARS.

12 YEARS OLD AND SHE STILL DOESN'T KNOW MY NAME IS JAMES!

JOKE 270

Q: CAN FEBRUARY MARCH?

A: NOPE! BUT APRIL MAY!

JOKE 271

Q: WHAT DO YOU CALL A GUY WITH A RUBBER TOE?

Q: ROBERTO.

JOKE 272

INTERVIEWER: OK, SO WHERE DO YOU SEE YOURSELF IN FIVE YEARS?

APPLICANT: PERSONALLY, I THINK MY BIGGEST FLAW IS LISTENING.

JOKE 273

Q: WHAT KIND OF SHOES DO BANANAS WEAR?

A: SLIPPERS.

JOKE 274

TALKING PARROT FOR SALE!

BECAUSE YESTERDAY THE LITTLE GUY TRIED TO SELL ME!

JOKE 275

Q: WHAT DO YOU CALL A SHEEP WITHOUT LEGS?

A: A CLOUD.

JOKE 276

Q: JOE HAS 20 CANDY BARS. HE EATS 15. WHAT DOES HE HAVE NOW?

A: DIABETES. JOE HAS DIABETES.

JOKE 277

Q: WHAT DOES A STOPWATCH DO WHEN IT'S HUNGRY?

A: IT GOES BACK FOUR SECONDS!

JOKE 278

Q: DID YOU HEAR ABOUT THE CLAUSTROPHOBIC SUPERNOVA?

A: IT REALLY NEEDED SOME SPACE.

JOKE 279

Q: HAVE YOU HEARD ABOUT THE CAMPGROUND FIRE?

A: IT WAS IN TENTS.

JOKE 280

Q: WHAT IS THE AWARD FOR BEING THE BEST DENTAL HYGIENIST?

A: A PLAQUE.

JOKE 281

Q: WHY DID THE TEACHER LOVE HER WHITEBOARD?

A: BECAUSE IT WAS JUST REMARKABLE!

JOKE 282

Q: WHY ARE THERE TWO DOORS ON CHICKEN COOPS?

A: BECAUSE IF THEY HAD FOUR DOORS, THEY WOULD BE CHICKEN SEDANS.

JOKE 283

Q: WHAT DID THE LEFT EYE SAY TO THE RIGHT?

A: BETWEEN YOU AND ME, SOMETHING SMELLS!

JOKE 284

Q: DID YOU HEAR ABOUT THE ACTRESS WHO FELL THROUGH THE FLOORBOARDS?

A: SHE WAS GOING THROUGH A STAGE.

JOKE 285

PATIENT: HEY DOC, I AM STARTING TO FORGET THINGS.

DOCTOR: WHEN DID IT START?

PATIENT: WHEN DID WHAT START?

JOKE 286

MY WIFE SCREAMED, "YOU HAVEN'T LISTENED TO ANYTHING I'VE SAID, HAVE YOU?!?"

WHAT A STRANGE WAY TO START A CONVERSATION.

JOKE 287

Q: WHY ARE SPACE ROCKS MORE DELICIOUS THAN EARTH ROCKS?

A: BECAUSE THEY ARE METEOR.

JOKE 288

Q: WHAT DID ONE PICKLE SAY TO THE OTHER PICKLE?

A: DILL WITH IT.

JOKE 289

Q: HOW DO PROFESSIONAL ATHLETES STAY COOL?

A: THEY ARE ALWAYS SURROUNDED BY FANS.

JOKE 290

Q: WHY DOES WALDO LOVE TO WEAR STIPES?

A: BECAUSE HE CAN'T STAND TO BE SPOTTED!

JOKE 291

I HAVE A GREAT JOKE ABOUT CONSTRUCTION.

I'M STILL WORKING ON IT.

JOKE 292

Q: HOW CAN YOU TELL IF THE OCEAN IS FRIENDLY?

A: IT WAVES!

JOKE 293

Q: WHAT DOES A MARCHING BAND INSTRUCTOR BRUSH HIS TEETH WITH?

A: A TUBA TOOTHPASTE.

JOKE 294

Q: WHY DID THE MECHANIC RUN OUT OF MUFFLERS?

A: BECAUSE HIS SUPPLY WAS EXHAUSTED.

JOKE 295

SON: I'LL CALL YOU LATER.

DAD: DON'T CALL ME LATER, CALL ME DAD!

JOKE 296

Q: WHY WAS THE TRAFFIC LIGHT EMBARRASSED?

A: BECAUSE EVERYONE WATCHED HER CHANGE!

JOKE 297

Q: WHAT IS AT THE BOTTOM OF THE OCEAN AND ALWAYS SHIVERING?

A: A NERVOUS WRECK.

JOKE 298

Q: WHO INVENTED THE ROUND TABLE?

A: SIR CUMFERENCE!

JOKE 299

I GOT THIS NEW DEODORANT.

THE INSTRUCTIONS SAY, "REMOVE CAP AND PUSH UP BOTTOM".

I CAN'T REALLY WALK, BUT WHEN I FART IT SMELLS GREAT.

JOKE 300

I HAVE THIS SPECIAL TALENT. I CAN ALWAYS GUESS WHAT IS INSIDE A WRAPPED PRESENT.

IT'S A GIFT.

JOKE 301

Q: WHY DON'T PEPPERS HAVE FRIENDS?

A: BECAUSE THEY GET JALAPENO BUSINESS.

JOKE 302

Q: WHAT DO POLITICIANS AND DIRTY DIAPERS HAVE IN COMMON?

A: BOTH SHOULD BE CHANGED REGULARLY, AND FOR THE SAME REASON!

JOKE 303

Q: WHY ARE SKUNKS ROMANTIC?

A: BECAUSE THEY ARE VERY SCENT-IMENTAL.

JOKE 304

I TOLD MY WIFE SHE DREW ON HER EYEBROWS TOO HIGH.

SHE SEEMED SURPRISED.

JOKE 305

Q: HOW MUCH DO PIRATES PAY FOR CORN ON THE COB?

A: A BUCCANEER.

JOKE 306

Q: WHAT DO YOU CALL A BLIND DEER?

A: NO-EYE-DEER.

JOKE 307

WIFE TO MOTHER: MY HUSBAND IS MAKING ME SO MAD! I AM COMING TO LIVE WITH YOU.

MOTHER TO WIFE: NO. HE SHOULD PAY FOR HIS MISTAKES! I AM COMING TO LIVE WITH YOU.

JOKE 308

Q: WHY ARE FISH SO EASY TO WEIGH?

A: BECAUSE THEY COME WITH THEIR OWN SCALES!

JOKE 309

Q: WHAT IS GREEN AND HAS CLAWS?

A: BROCCOLI. I LIED ABOUT THE CLAWS.

JOKE 310

Q: WHAT DID THE TWO PIECES OF BREAD SAY ABOUT THEIR RELATIONSHIP?

A: IT WAS LOAF AT FIRST SIGHT.

JOKE 311

Q: WHAT IS THE BEST WAY TO TRACK WILL SMITH IN THE SNOW?

A: FOLLOW THE FRESH PRINTS.

JOKE 312

Q: WHY WAS THE ARENA SO WINDY?

A: IT WAS FULL OF FANS.

JOKE 313

DOCTOR: YOU ARE MORBIDLY OBESE.

PATIENT: I WANT A SECOND OPINION!

DOCTOR: NO PROBLEM, YOU ARE ALSO UGLY.

JOKE 314

Q: WHAT SHOULD YOU GIVE A SICK CITRUS TREE?

A: LEMON-AID!

JOKE 315

THE ROTATION OF THE EARTH REALLY MAKES MY DAY.

JOKE 316

Q: DO YOU KNOW WHAT REALLY MAKES ME SMILE?

A: MY FACIAL MUSCLES.

JOKE 317

MAN: YOU ARE THE MOST BEAUTIFUL WOMAN IN THE WORLD!

WOMAN: WHATEVER, YOU ARE JUST TRYING TO GET ME IN BED.

MAN: AND SMART, TOO!

JOKE 318

Q: WHAT DID ADAM SAY TO HIS WIFE THE DAY BEFORE CHRISTMAS?

A: IT'S CHRISTMAS, EVE!

JOKE 319

I TOLD MY MOTHER IN LAW SHE HAD TOO MUCH BOTOX.

SHE DIDN'T SEEM SURPRISED.

JOKE 320

HAVE YOU HEARD ABOUT THE BAR ON THE MOON?

GREAT DRINKS. NO ATMOSPHERE!

JOKE 321

I LEFT MY EX-GIRLFRIEND BECAUSE SHE WAS SO OBSESSED WITH COUNTING.

I WONDER WHAT SHE IS UP TO NOW.

JOKE 322

KID: DAD, CAN YOU PUT MY SHOES ON?

DAD: NOPE, I DON'T THINK THEY WILL FIT ME!

JOKE 323

MY WIFE IS ALWAYS FRUSTRATED THAT I HAVE NO SENSE OF DIRECTION.

SO, I PACKED UP MY STUFF AND RIGHT.

JOKE 324

Q: WHY WAS THE CHICKEN A BAD REFEREE?

A: HE KEPT OVERCALLING FOWLS.

JOKE 325

I HAVE HEARD THAT PEOPLE PICK THEIR NOSE.

BUT I WAS JUST BORN WITH THE ONE I HAVE.

JOKE 326

Q: WHAT DID THE ACCOUNTANT SAY AFTER A FULL DAY OF WORK?

A: THIS IS TAXING!

JOKE 327

COMIC SANS AND TIMES NEW ROMAN WALK INTO A BAR.

THE BARTENDER YELLS, "GET OUT OF HERE! WE DON'T SERVE YOUR TYPE!"

JOKE 328

Q: WHY ARE PIGLETS BAD AT SPORTS?

A: BECAUSE THEY ARE ALWAYS HOGGING THE BALL.

JOKE 329

I HAVE BEEN CONSIDERING TAKING UP MEDITATION.

IT MUST BE BETTER THAN SITTING AROUND DOING NOTHING.

JOKE 330

I INVENTED A NEW WORD.

PLAGIARISM!

JOKE 331

Q: HOW DOES THE MOON CUT HIS HAIR?

A: ECLIPSE IT.

JOKE 332

SOMEONE JUST THREW MILK AT ME. HOW DAIRY?!

JOKE 333

Q: WHY DID THE CUCUMBER BLUSH?

A: BECAUSE HE SAW THE SALAD DRESSING.

JOKE 334

Q: WHAT DO YOU CALL AN UNDERCOVER NOODLE?

A: AN IMPASTA.

JOKE 335

A MOTHER ASKED HER SON, "BILLY, DO YOU THINK I AM A GOOD MOM?"

SON: "MY NAME IS SAM."

JOKE 336

Q: WHAT DO YOU CALL A LAMB DRESSED AS A ROCKSTAR FOR HALLOWEEN?

A: BAAAAAAD TO THE BONE.

JOKE 337

Q: WHY DON'T ANTS EVER GET SICK?

A: BECAUSE THEY HAVE ANTY-BODIES.

JOKE 338

OH MAN, I CAN'T BELIEVE I FORGOT TO GO TO THE GYM TODAY!

THAT'S 8 YEARS IN A ROW!

JOKE 339

Q: WHAT DID THE MIME SAY TO HIS AUDIENCE?

A: NOTHING.

JOKE 340

Q: DID I TELL YOU ABOUT WHEN I FELL IN LOVE DURING A BACKFLIP?

A: I FELL HEELS OVER HEAD!

JOKE 341

Q: WHAT DO YOU CALL A SLEEPING BULL?

A: A BULL-DOZER

JOKE 342

Q: WHAT DID THE PROFESSOR DO WITH THE REPORT ON CHEESE?

A: SHE GRATED IT.

JOKE 343

SINGING IN THE BATHTUB IS FUN UNTIL YOU GET SHAMPOO IN YOUR MOUTH.

THEN IT BECOMES A SOAP OPERA.

JOKE 344

JUST AS I SUSPECTED.

SOMEONE HAS BEEN ADDING FERTILIZER TO MY GARDEN.

THE PLOT THICKENS.

JOKE 345

I JUST STARTED A BOOK ABOUT ANTI-GRAVITY.

IT IS IMPOSSIBLE TO PUT DOWN!

JOKE 346

TWO DONKEYS ARE CONSIDERING CROSSING A ROAD.

ONE SAYS, "NO WAY. LOOK AT WHAT HAPPENED TO THE ZEBRA!"

JOKE 347

Q: WHAT DO YOU CALL A FISH WITH ONE EYE MISSING?

A: A F-SHHH

JOKE 348

Q: WHY ARE PIGS BAD AT KEEPING SECRETS?

A: BECAUSE THEY SQUEAL.

JOKE 349

Q: WHAT DID THE GOOSE SAY WHEN SHE BOUGHT LIPSTICK?

A: PUT IT ON MY BILL

JOKE 350

I KNOW MONEY CAN'T BUY YOU HAPPINESS.

BUT I WOULD BE A LOT MORE COMFORTABLE CRYING IN A NEW SPORTS CAR THAN A BIKE!

JOKE 351

Q: WHAT DO YOU CALL A BELT MADE OF CLOCKS?

A: A WAIST OF TIME.

JOKE 352

Q: WHAT DID THE JUICER SAY TO THE ORANGE DURING QUARANTINE?

A: I CAN'T WAIT TO SQUEEZE YOU!

JOKE 353

Q: HOW MANY TICKLES DOES IT TAKE TO MAKE AN OCTOPUS LAUGH?

A: TEN TICKLES.

JOKE 354

Q: WHY DID THE CHEF THROW BUTTER OUT OF THE WINDOW?

A: HE WANTED TO SEE A BUTTERFLY.

JOKE 355

Q: WHAT DO HILLBILLIES DRINK FROM?

A: HICCUPS.

JOKE 356

Q: WHAT IS THE BEST WAY TO CATCH A BRA?

A: WITH A BOOBY TRAP.

JOKE 357

Q: WHY DID ADELE CROSS THE ROAD?

A: TO SAY HELLO FROM THE OTHER SIDE.

JOKE 358

"HEY GRANDMA, WHY DON'T YOU HAVE LIFE INSURANCE?"

"SO, YOU CAN TRULY BE SAD WHEN I DIE!"

JOKE 359

Q: WHAT DO YOU CALL A DAIRY COW DURING AN EARTHQUAKE?

A: MILKSHAKE.

JOKE 360

I HAD A NECK BRACE FITTED YEARS AGO.

I HAVE NEVER LOOKED BACK SINCE!

JOKE 361

Q: HOW DOES A MUMMY START A LETTER?

A: TOMB IT MAY CONCERN...

JOKE 362

Q: WHY DID THE SINGER GO SAILING?

A: SHE WANTED TO HIT THE HIGH CS.

JOKE 363

HOSTESS: SORRY ABOUT YOUR WAIT.

DAD: ARE YOU SAYING THAT I'M FAT?

JOKE 364

Q: WHAT VEGETABLE DOES A SAILOR AVOID AT ALL COSTS?

A: LEEK

JOKE 365

HAVE I TOLD YOU ABOUT THE TIME MY DOG ATE THE SCRABBLE TILES?

HE KEPT LEAVING ME LITTLE MESSAGES ALL AROUND THE HOUSE!

Made in the USA
Middletown, DE
17 June 2024